Gute Nacht, mein Liebling!
Goodnight, My Love!

Shelley Admont

Illustrationen von Samir Boumsik

www.kidkiddos.com
Copyright©2015 by S.A.Publishing ©2017 by KidKiddos Books Ltd.
support@kidkiddos.com

All rights reserved. No part of this book may be reproduced in any form or by any electronic or mechanical means, including information storage and retrieval systems, without written permission from the publisher or author, except in the case of a reviewer, who may quote brief passages embodied in critical articles or in a review.

Alle Rechte vorbehalten. Kein Teil dieses Buches darf in irgendeiner Form oder durch irgendwelche elektronischen oder mechanischen Mitteln, einschließlich Informationen Regalbediengeräte schriftlich beim Verlag, mit Ausnahme von einem Rezensenten, kurze Passagen in einer Bewertung zitieren darf reproduziert, ohne Erlaubnis.

First edition, 2018
Edited by Martha Robert
Translated from English by Tess Parthum
Aus dem Englischen übersetzt von Tess Parthum
German editing by Anne-Kristin Beinhauer

Library and Archives Canada Cataloguing in Publication
Goodnight, My Love! (German English Bilingual Edition)/ Shelley Admont
ISBN: 978-1-5259-0999-3 paperback
ISBN: 978-1-5259-1000-5 hardcover
ISBN: 978-1-5259-0998-6 eBook

Please note that the German and English versions of the story have been written to be as close as possible. However, in some cases they differ in order to accommodate nuances and fluidity of each language.

Although the author and the publisher have made every effort to ensure the accuracy and completeness of information contained in this book, we assume no responsibility for errors, inaccuracies, omission, inconsistency, or consequences from such information.

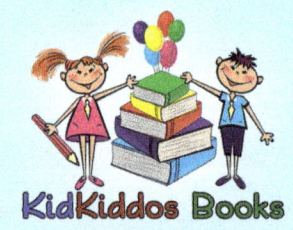

Zeit, ins Bett zu gehen, mein Sohn. Putz dir die Zähne und zieh deinen Schlafanzug an. Schlüpf ins Bett und ich werde dir eine Geschichte vorlesen", sagte Papa.

"Time for bed, son. Brush your teeth and put on your pajamas. Climb into bed, and I will read you a story," said Dad.

Als Alex ins Bett geschlüpft war, las ihm sein Papa eine Geschichte vor. Danach deckte er ihn zu und beugte sich nach vorn.

When Alex had climbed into bed, his dad read him a story. After that, he tucked him in and leaned over.

„Gute Nacht, mein Sohn. Gute Nacht, Liebling. Ich hab' dich lieb", sagte er.

"Goodnight, son. Goodnight, dear. I love you," he said.

„Ich hab' dich auch lieb, Papi, aber ich kann jetzt nicht schlafen", sagte Alex.

"I love you too, Daddy, but I can't sleep right now," said Alex.

„Warum, mein Sohn? Was ist los?", fragte Papa.

"Why, son? What's wrong?" asked Dad.

„Ich brauche zuerst noch einen Schluck Wasser", antwortete Alex.

"I need a drink of water first," Alex answered.

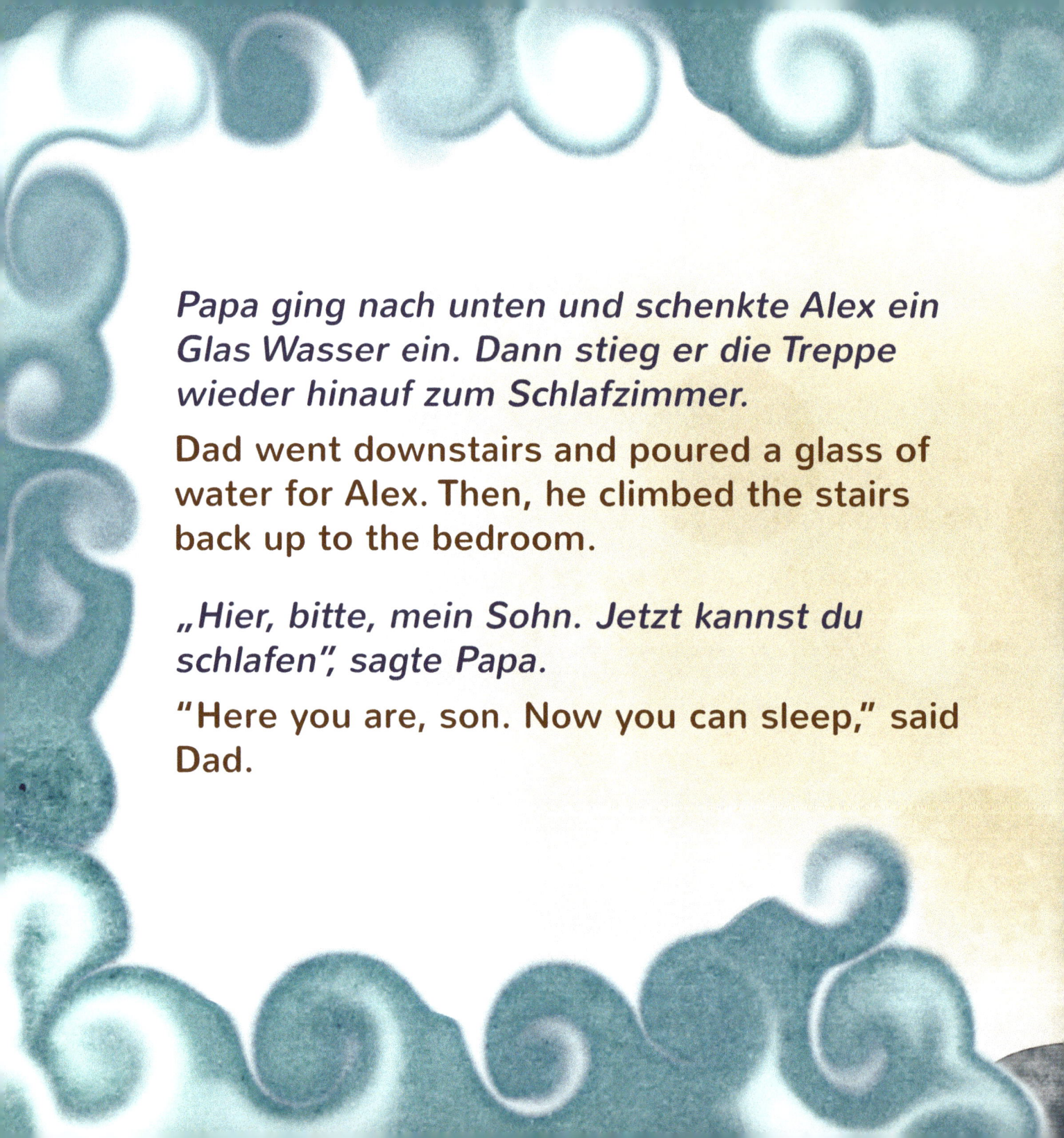

Papa ging nach unten und schenkte Alex ein Glas Wasser ein. Dann stieg er die Treppe wieder hinauf zum Schlafzimmer.

Dad went downstairs and poured a glass of water for Alex. Then, he climbed the stairs back up to the bedroom.

„Hier, bitte, mein Sohn. Jetzt kannst du schlafen", sagte Papa.

"Here you are, son. Now you can sleep," said Dad.

Alex trank das Glas Wasser und legte sich wieder hin. Sein Papa deckte ihn zu und beugte sich nach vorn.

Alex drank the glass of water and lay back down. His dad tucked him in and leaned over.

„Gute Nacht, mein Sohn. Gute Nacht, Liebling. Ich hab' dich lieb", sagte er.

"Goodnight, son. Goodnight, dear. I love you," he said.

„Ich hab' dich auch lieb, Papi, aber ich kann jetzt nicht schlafen."

"I love you too, Daddy, but I can't sleep right now."

„Warum, mein Sohn? Was ist los?", fragte Papa.

"Why, son? What's wrong?" asked Dad.

„Ich brauche meinen Teddybären", antwortete Alex.

"I need my teddy bear," answered Alex.

Papa durchquerte das Zimmer und holte einen blauen Teddybären.

Dad walked across the room and picked up a blue teddy bear.

Er nahm ihn und gab ihn Alex.

He brought it back and gave it to Alex.

„Nicht diesen, Papi. Ich brauche den grauen Teddy", sagte Alex.

"Not this one, Daddy. I need the grey teddy bear," said Alex.

Papa lachte. Er ging nach unten, um einen grauen Teddybären von der Couch zu holen. Dann stieg er wieder die Treppe hinauf zum Zimmer seines Sohnes.

Dad laughed. He went downstairs to get a grey teddy bear from the couch. Then, he climbed the stairs back up to his son's room again.

„*Hier ist dein Teddybär. Jetzt kannst du schlafen*", *sagte Papa.*

"Here is your teddy bear. Now you can sleep," said Dad.

„*Danke, Papi!*", *sagte Alex.*

"Thank you, Daddy!" said Alex.

Papa deckte seinen Sohn und den Teddybären zu und beugte sich nach vorne.

Dad tucked in his son and the grey teddy bear and leaned over.

„Gute Nacht, mein Sohn. Gute Nacht, Liebling. Ich hab' dich lieb", sagte er.

"Goodnight, son. Goodnight, dear. I love you," he said.

„Ich hab' dich auch lieb, Papi, aber ich kann immer noch nicht schlafen", sagte Alex erneut.

"I love you too, Daddy, but I still can't sleep yet," said Alex again.

„Warum, mein Sohn? Was ist los?", fragte Papa.

"Why, son? What's wrong?" asked Dad.

„Ach, ich weiß nicht, wovon ich träumen soll", antwortete Alex.

"Well, I don't know what to dream about," answered Alex.

„Wenn du alles sein könntest, Alex, was wärst du dann?"

"If you could be anything at all, Alex, what would you be?"

„Ich wäre ein Vogel und würde im sanften Wind schweben", antwortete Alex.

"I'd be a bird and float on the breeze," answered Alex.

„Was für ein schöner Traum, mein Sohn!",
sagte Papa.

"What a beautiful dream, son!" said Dad.

„Und was passiert dann?", fragte Alex.

"But, what will happen next?" asked Alex.

„Zuerst werden du und ich durch die weichen, flauschigen Wolken emporsteigen. Die Sonne wird unsere Federn mit ihrem sanften, rosaroten Schein wärmen", sagte Papa.

"First, you and I will soar through the soft, fluffy clouds. The sun will warm our feathers with its gentle, pink glow," said Dad.

„Der Sonnenaufgang ist schön, Papi!", sagte Alex. Papa nickte.

"The sunrise is beautiful, Daddy!" said Alex. Dad nodded.

„Dann werden wir über die kalten, grauen Berge gleiten und am stillen Wald vorbei", sagte Papa.

"Next, we will glide over the cool, gray mountains and past the quiet forest," said Dad.

„Anschließend werden wir im warmen Wasser des Meeres schwimmen gehen. Die Brise wird sanft und salzig sein, während wir auf den ruhigen, blauen Wellen dahin treiben", sagte Papa.

"Then, we will go for a swim in the warm waters of the sea. The breeze will be gentle and salty as we float atop the calm, blue waves," said Dad.

„Was passiert dann?", fragte Alex mit einem großen Gähnen.

"What happens next?" asked Alex with a big yawn.

„Wir landen auf den weichen, weißen Wellenkissen", sagte Papa leise.

"We'll land on the fluffy, white cloud-pillows," said Dad quietly.

Papa sah den schlafenden Alex an und beugte sich nach vorn.

Dad looked at Alex sleeping and leaned over.

„Gute Nacht, mein Sohn. Gute Nacht, Liebling", sagte Papa. Dann gab er seinem Sohn einen Kuss auf die Stirn. „Ich werde dich immer lieb haben. Gute Nacht!"

"Goodnight, son. Goodnight, dear. I love you," said Dad. Then, he gave his son a kiss on his forehead. "I will always love you. Goodnight!"

www.ingramcontent.com/pod-product-compliance
Lightning Source LLC
LaVergne TN
LVHW072052060526
838200LV00061B/4721